How
Jesus
Cares

31 devotions about Christ
and his love for you

SINCLAIR B. FERGUSON

TRUTHFORLIFE®
CF4•K

10 9 8 7 6 5 4 3 2

Copyright © 2022 Sinclair B. Ferguson
Hardback 978-1-5271-0859-2
E-book 978-1-5271-0928-5

Reprinted in 2022
by Christian Focus Publications,
Geanies House, Fearn, Tain, Ross-shire,
IV20 1TW, Scotland, U.K.
www.christianfocus.com
with
Truth For Life
P.O. Box 398000
Cleveland, Ohio 44139
truthforlife.org

Cover design and page layout by
James Amour
Printed and bound by Gutenberg, Malta

CONTENTS

Introduction

If you go to church or Sunday school, maybe you have heard grown-ups speaking about how important it is to spend time each day with the Lord Jesus, and to think about him.

I don't know about you, but I find it hard just to sit down and think. Sometimes my head feels empty. But then, at other times, it feels as though there are too many things to think about! So, it's not easy just to sit down and say to yourself, 'I am going to think about Jesus for the next five minutes.'

What helps me is when I have something to think about—something that makes me think! So, reading a book helps me. Or if someone asks a question. It's a bit like starting the engine in the car—something needs to turn the key or press the starter button. You read and then you start thinking. Or you hear the question and you try to work out the answer—so you start thinking! I have tried to put these two things together in this book. I hope that reading it will start you thinking about Jesus. In addition, since each of its chapters begins with a question, I hope that will help you think even more about him. Don't forget to ask for his help by using the prayers.

When I was at school we hardly ever spoke in class. We spent a lot of time writing. So I find writing helps me to think. Not everybody likes writing. But if you do, why don't you keep a little book and write down your thoughts about Jesus while you are reading this book? Who knows, maybe one day you'll write a book like this one!

But until you write your own book, I hope you will enjoy the one I have written for you!

Sinclair B. Ferguson

1. RUNNING THE RACE

Lord Jesus,
help me to think about you, learn
more about you, and love you today.

READ: HEBREWS 12:1-2

Have you ever run in a race? What did it feel like? If you run in a race it can be hard going and tiring!

The Bible tells us that the Christian life is like a long race. In Hebrews Chapter 11, we read about Moses and Daniel. Moses suffered a great deal. Pharaoh was against him. Even his own Hebrew people criticised him. Daniel was thrown into a lion's den because he worshipped the one true God. His friends, Shadrach, Meshach and Abednego, were put in a fiery furnace because they would not worship the king's statue. They wanted to trust in the Lord and to serve him.

These men ran the race of faith—even although it must have felt very lonely sometimes.

You may feel that you are running this race all on your own. Perhaps there are no other Christians in your class at school. Maybe you are the only one in your family who loves Jesus? But remember this, all over the world there are millions of people who are following Jesus. They are running the Christian race, just like you, because it is the greatest race in the world.

If we run the Christian race we need to get rid of things that hold us back. These are obstacles. Hebrews Chapter 12 tells us to throw away things that keep us from following Jesus. Would you run a race with a heavy rucksack on your back? Of course not! Well, just as there are things that slow you down in a running race, there are things that get in the way in the Christian race too.

One of these things is greed. Do you spend lots of time thinking about the things that you want to get? We need to get rid of greed. Lies, bad temper and pride hold us back too. We can't run the Christian race if we hold on to these things. The good news is that the Lord Jesus promises to help us get rid of them if we ask him. It may not be easy, but the Lord Jesus will help us so that we can run the Christian race and follow him. A marathon race is twenty-six miles. It is the longest of all the races in the Olympic games. It commemorates a man who ran to Athens in order to tell the people there that the Persian army had been defeated at the Battle of Marathon.

Following Jesus is like a marathon. That is why we need to have the Holy Spirit to help us. There will be times when we don't have the strength to keep going. But the Lord Jesus says, 'When you are weak, I will come and make you strong' (See Romans 8:26; 2 Corinthians 12:9).

There are prizes for everybody who runs in the Christian race. We are told to keep our eyes on the finishing tape. One day the Christian race will be over at the end of our life on earth. But when we finish, Jesus will be there to greet us. He will have a prize for us.

Part of this prize will be that Jesus will give us our own special name (See Revelation 2:17)! It will be the greatest prize in the world! Let's run to get that prize. Jesus will help us all the way.

Lord Jesus

Thank you that you have run this race before us, right to the cross. Thank you that you died for us. Please send your Holy Spirit into our hearts so that we will be with you forever. We pray this in your name.

Amen.

2. WHERE DO YOU BELONG?

Lord Jesus,
help me to think about you, learn
more about you, and love you today.

READ: JOHN 15:18-19

Have you ever been asked the question, 'Where do you belong?' You might reply, 'I belong to Glasgow,' or 'I live in England.' Perhaps you come from another country like America or New Zealand.

If someone asks you, 'Who do you belong to?' would you say, 'I belong to my mum and dad'? A married person would say, 'I belong to my husband' or 'I belong to my wife.'

If you move to a new town you might feel that you don't really belong. Things are different. Maybe someone will tell you, 'You don't belong here. You're not one of us! We're not going to play with you.'

That can really hurt!

Sometimes people don't like you when you belong to the Lord Jesus. Maybe they know that you go to church. They may even be nasty to you.

Jesus says, 'Whenever that happens, remember that you belong to me. They do this to you because they don't love me either. It's because you belong to me that they are being mean to you. It's because you love me that they hate you. It's because you want to follow me that these things are happening. Trust me and I will take care of everything' (See Matthew 10:22; Matthew 24:9; Mark 13:13; Luke 10:5-6; Luke 21:7).

Maybe one day some of the people who have been nasty to you will actually come to you and say, 'Can you help me to trust Jesus in the way you do?'

So, whenever you feel that because you belong to Jesus, you don't belong with your pals, remember this:

Jesus is with you always. You always belong to him!

Let's pray that the Lord Jesus will help us to be faithful to him. Then through our lives, he will help others to trust him too.

Loving Heavenly Father

We know that you love us. You understand how painful it is when we feel we don't belong. Sometimes our friends don't want to belong to us because we belong to you. Please help us to trust you. We ask these things in Jesus' name.

Amen.

3. A NEW WORD

Lord Jesus,
help me to think about you, learn
more about you, and love you today.

READ: ACTS 11:19 – 26

Do you like to discover new words and what they mean? What do you do when you come across a word that you don't know? Do you ask someone what it means? But what if the word hasn't been invented yet, what would you do then?

Acts 11:26 tells us, 'The disciples were first called Christians in Antioch.' That means that it was in the city of Antioch that somebody thought up a new word to describe the followers of Jesus.

The new word they thought up was the word 'Christian' which means 'Christ's one'.

When I come across a word and I don't know what it means, I look it up in my dictionary. There are many different words in a dictionary – and each one of them has its own meaning.

Perhaps your friends at school or football club don't really know what the word 'Christian' means. How are they going to find out?

They might not look up a dictionary. Perhaps your friends don't ever read the Bible. But they could find out, couldn't they? If you are a Christian they could find out what a Christian is like by looking at you!

If they watched the things that you said and did, they would be able to learn what it really means to be a Christian. Instead of having to read a dictionary, they could come to you and say, 'How do I become a Christian like you?' Wouldn't that be amazing?

That's exactly what happened in Antioch. The people in Antioch looked at the Christians and saw that they loved Jesus and that Jesus loved them. So they gave them the name 'Christ's Ones'. They knew that these people belonged to Jesus and followed him.

Let's pray that we will show our friends and family what a Christian is through our words and actions.

Lord Jesus

We thank you that you speak to us through your Word in the Bible. By your Spirit, you are able to make us more and more like you. May our friends begin to see your love and your power in our lives and want to become Christians too. We pray this in your name.

Amen.

4. NICKNAMES

Lord Jesus,
help me to think about you, learn
more about you, and love you today.

READ: ACTS 4:32–36

Do you have a nickname? Do some of your friends have nicknames? What are they?

In Acts 4: 36 a man called Joseph was given a nickname. He was a disciple of Jesus. Later on, he became a close friend of the Apostle Paul. His real name was Joseph. He was originally from Cyprus, an island in the Mediterranean Sea, but he had moved to Jerusalem.

> ... Joseph, who was also called by the apostles Barnabas (which means son of encouragement), a Levite, a native of Cyprus ... (Acts 4:36 ESV).

Joseph wasn't called 'Joseph' for long. The apostles gave him a nickname – 'Barnabas'. It means 'Son of

Encouragement' because he was always helping and encouraging people.

If you had asked him, 'What's your name?' he would have said, 'My name is Joseph Levi but my friends call me Barnabas.'

Are you ever called something different by your friends at school from what you're called at home? Michael at home – Mike at school, for example. Sometimes Mum and Dad don't like your name to be shortened. Perhaps you're called Jonny at school, but Mum and Dad say, 'Jonathan' which is quite a mouthful.

Now I know what it's like to have a name that is a bit of a mouthful. My name is 'Sinclair B. Ferguson'. The B stands for my middle name, 'Buchanan'. My mum gave me these names for two different reasons. One of the reasons was because she thought nobody would ever shorten or change the name 'Sinclair' into something else. (She was wrong!)

I'm sure Barnabas' mother called him 'Joseph' but maybe his pals at school called him 'Joe'. However, when he became a Christian everybody called him 'Barnabas' because he was always helping them and encouraging them. That was why they called him 'Son of Encouragement' – that's what 'Barnabas' means.

Choose a nickname for yourself from the list of words in Galatians 5:22-23.

> But the fruit of the Spirit is love, joy, peace, longsuffering, kindness, goodness, faithfulness, gentleness, self-control.

Then ask the Lord Jesus, 'Lord Jesus, make me like that nickname'. What name will you choose? Write this name down and say, 'Lord Jesus, help me to be like that so that I'll have a nickname that you alone know.'

Do you remember how Revelation 2:17 says that Jesus will give a nickname to every Christian that only they will know? What nickname would you like Jesus to give you?

Lord Jesus

We thank you that Barnabas helped and encouraged his fellow Christians. May we have good nicknames too. Help us to set our hearts on being like you so that we can be your servants. We pray this for your sake.

Amen.

5. LEARN FROM A FARMER

Lord Jesus,
help me to think about you, learn
more about you, and love you today.

READ: JAMES 5:7–12

Are you patient? Or are you one of those people who just can't wait for something to happen – like a birthday or the end of the day at school?

James 5:7 (ESV) tells us to wait patiently for the return of the Lord Jesus.

> *Be patient, therefore, brothers, until the*
> *coming of the Lord. See how the farmer*
> *waits for the precious fruit of the earth,*
> *being patient about it, until it receives the*
> *early and the late rains.*

What does it mean to wait patiently? Well, farmers have to do this all the time. They wait for their valuable crops to grow and ripen. They patiently let the rain do its slow but sure work. A farmer sows his seed, comes home, has his dinner, goes to bed, gets up in the morning, waits for the rain, goes to bed, goes to work in the morning, waits for the rain, day after day after day. Slowly harvest time comes. A farmer needs to be very patient.

The Bible says that we are to be patient too. We are to wait patiently for the return of the Lord Jesus Christ.

James uses two different words for being patient. The first word is *makrothumeō*. It is made up of two Greek words, *thumos* which means 'anger' and *makros* which means 'long'. So the word *makrothumeō* is used when a person takes a long, long, long, long time to get irritated. In other words they are a patient person, like a farmer.

The farmer isn't sitting at his breakfast saying, 'I will make God hurry up with those rains.' He knows he must wait for God to send the rain so that there will be a harvest. While he waits he keeps working.

The other word James uses is *hupomonē*. This word means 'to remain or stay underneath'. What James was saying was that we are to 'wait', to 'wait underneath'.

Have you ever seen the Olympic weightlifters in the 'Snatch and Grab' competition? They pick up enormous weights and hold them above their heads. That's what this word *hupomonē* means. It means that when things are heavy or difficult, you're able to take the strain! To be a Christian, you need *hupomonē*. You need to know that God is producing a harvest of good things in your life. If you have *hupomonē*, even when things get bad and sore, you are able to wait for God to produce the harvest.

If you are a Christian, God is preparing a harvest for your life. He has plans for what he wants you to do. He'll maybe take you all over the world to serve the Lord Jesus. But first we must learn to trust him, and to wait. Because one day he's going to come back for us!

Lord Jesus

We thank you that you took the pain of the cross. Thank you for being so patient with us and helping us to trust in you and love you. Help us to always be patient and to look forward to your coming again. We ask this in your name.

Amen.

Lord Jesus,
help me to think about you, learn
more about you, and love you today.

READ: GENESIS 20:1-5

Do you know what a coward is? A coward is somebody who is afraid to do things they know they ought to.

Abraham was a wonderful man of faith. But sometimes he was brave and sometimes he was a coward.

He was brave when God said, 'I want you to leave your home and go to a new place. I am not going to tell you where this is. You will have to trust me.'

Abraham trusted God, got all his family together and they set off on their camels. At that point Abraham was very strong and brave. (This story is in Genesis 12.)

However, sometimes Abraham was a coward. One time Abraham and his wife, Sarah, met King Abimilech.

Sarah was very beautiful. Abraham was worried that if other men saw his beautiful wife they might kill him and steal her.

So, when Abraham met King Abimilech, he told him that Sarah was his sister and not his wife. What a coward! Just then all kinds of strange and really frightening things began to happen because Abraham had lied, instead of being a courageous witness for God. (This part of Abraham's story is in Genesis 20.)

Perhaps you feel a bit frightened when somebody asks you, 'Do you go to Sunday school? Do you follow the Lord Jesus?'

Instead of saying 'Yes – I love Sunday school, and Yes, I follow the Lord Jesus', sometimes we get a bit wobbly inside and say only, 'Well, I have been at Sunday school. Oh yes, I have heard about Jesus.'

What are we going to do about our cowardly hearts? Well, we can say to the Lord Jesus 'I am just jelly inside. I don't know what is going to happen to me if I tell my friends that I love you and trust you.'

Jesus says, 'I will never, ever, ever, ever, leave you and I will be specially with you when you are scared. I will give you strength. Do not be afraid!' Tell Jesus that you need his help. He has promised that he will never, ever, leave you and he will always be with you.

Lord Jesus

You know what it is like to be afraid. We thank you that you conquered your fears and that you were faithful to your Father. We pray that you would help us to reach out to you, to trust in your promise, to live by your Word, and to be good witnesses to your grace. We pray this in your name.

Amen.

7. JUST DO IT!

*Lord Jesus,
help me to think about you, learn
more about you, and love you today.*

READ: JAMES 2:20–24

What is a Christian? What is the most important thing for a Christian to be?

There were some people in the early church who said that to be a real Christian you needed to do the things that the Jewish people did. You had to observe the holy days and be careful about the things that you could eat and not eat. People like Paul said, 'No. To be a Christian what we have to do is trust in the Lord Jesus, because he died to take away our sins.'

Some people said that they trusted in Jesus, but they didn't show it. They weren't obedient. They didn't do the things that the Lord Jesus said. So, James, Jesus' brother, reminded them of Abraham who had trusted God and had obeyed him.

God had wanted Abraham to show how much he trusted him by doing something that was hard. He told Abraham to take his only son, Isaac, and offer him up as a sacrifice. Because Abraham trusted in God, he obeyed him. However, just at the last minute God stopped Abraham and gave him a ram for the sacrifice instead. Abraham did not need to sacrifice his son. God did not want him to do that. Abraham had shown that he trusted in the Lord. (You can read this story in Genesis 22.)

When James told this story he was trying to help the first Christians to understand that when we trust in Jesus, then we will do the things he says. We will help people who are poor and needy. We will make friends with those who are lonely.

If we see people who are alone and don't befriend them, then we are not really trusting in Jesus. If we don't show love and care for people who are very poor, then we aren't really following Jesus. We're not really being Christian.

If we trust in Jesus we will want to do the things that Jesus tells us to do. After all, Jesus is the Son of God. He actually became a sacrifice for our sins when he died on the cross. Because he has loved us like that, we can trust him and obey him.

Lord Jesus

We trust you. Sometimes you ask us to show that we trust you by doing things that are hard. Please fill us with love for you and others so that we can serve you more. This we ask for your sake.

Amen.

8. A WICKED TONGUE

Lord Jesus,
help me to think about you, learn
more about you, and love you today.

READ: PSALM 10

Have you ever sucked a peppermint? What do you feel? Did you get the taste? It's strong. It's very strong! It's so strong it's the only thing you can taste! But how would a bad peppermint taste?

Psalm 10 was written by a man who was not being treated very nicely. People were giving him a hard time. He said: 'Trouble and evil are under the wicked man's tongue' (See verse 7).

Psalm 10 is talking about people who have trouble and evil under their tongues. They say and do evil. Perhaps there is somebody like that in your school. They know that you love the Lord Jesus and want to follow him. Underneath their tongues are the words, 'I hate Jesus.'

What do you do when you meet somebody with these words under their tongue? What do you do when someone is horrible to you because you love Jesus and want to follow him?

Here are some things you can do.

1. Speak to Jesus about it.
2. Remember the same things happened to Jesus. The reason it's happening to you is because you belong to Jesus and you love Jesus.
3. Remember Saul of Tarsus.

Saul of Tarsus? Why should we remember him? Saul felt a deep-down hatred for the Lord Jesus. He especially hated Stephen because Stephen loved Jesus so much. But one day Saul himself became a Christian. Jesus stopped him on the road to Damascus and Saul became one of his disciples. (You can read about this in Acts 9.)

Being a Christian today can be really tough. Our world is full of people who have stuck peppermints of evil under their tongues. But Jesus is able to keep us and to help us.

Lord Jesus

You have called us to be very brave. Some people don't love you and are mean to us. Thank you for always being near to us. Bless us with courage. Help us to be faithful to you and to love you. Please help all my friends to trust in you and to become your disciples. In your great name we pray.

Amen.

9. GROWING UP

*Lord Jesus,
help me to think about you, learn
more about you, and love you today.*

READ: LUKE 2:41-52

Are you the oldest in the family, apart from Dad or Mum? Do you think it's easier being the youngest or the oldest?

I had a big brother. I was the younger son and he was the elder. Sometimes it's not easy having a big brother or sister. They're bigger and they're stronger. As well as that, they are almost always the first to do things. When I was quite little, my big brother went to school before I did. I really wanted to go to school too because he was at school, but I had to wait.

My big brother always seemed to have more money than I had. And then he got to leave school before I did. He got a good job and he had a car before I did. One day one of my teachers told me that I would never be like my big brother! So I used to wish that I could grow up quicker! I wanted to be able to miss a year or two at school. Why couldn't I just grow up?

But there is absolutely nothing you can do to make yourself older, is there? You just cannot do it. You cannot make yourself grow up more quickly. You've got to take one day at a time.

However, you can grow up more quickly as a Christian. Luke 2: 52 says that Jesus grew up quickly. He became wise and he loved God very much.

> *And Jesus increased in wisdom and stature, and in favour with God and man* (Luke 2:52).

Here are some things that will help you to do this.

1. Get to know your Bible. Read it or ask someone to read it to you.
2. Speak to God in prayer and get to know him that way.
3. Serve him. Tell others about him. Love him. Do the things that he wants you to do. Trust him absolutely.

Will you think about these things? These are things that will really help you to grow and grow. You might grow so much that you'll be taller as a Christian than somebody who is much taller in height than you are.

Lord Jesus

We thank you that when you were a little boy you kept on growing. You grew in love for your Father. You knew him, served him and were obedient to him. Please help us to do this. Help us to grow tall as Christians. For your sake.

Amen.

10. WORDS THAT DON'T MAKE SENSE

Lord Jesus,
help me to think about you, learn
more about you, and love you today.

READ: ACTS 11:1–18

What would you think of someone who came up to you and said, 'Hurry up now! Slowly!'? It doesn't really make sense does it?

When you put two words together that actually mean opposite things like 'hurry' and 'slowly', this is called an *oxymoron*.

Do you know what a 'moron' is? It means somebody who is really stupid. 'Oxy' comes from a Greek word that means sharp. If someone describes you as being 'sharp' they usually mean you are clever. They are certainly not describing you as being stupid.

So 'Oxy', which means sharp and 'Moron', which means stupid don't really go together. Just like 'Hurry up – slowly.'

An oxymoron is when you put two words together that don't really belong.

Peter used an oxymoron in Acts 11:8. He said: 'Not so, Lord!' Do you see the two words in this sentence that don't belong together? 'Not' and 'Lord.' That's like saying, 'No, Lord.' These words just don't go together.

Peter should have known not to use these words. It wasn't the first time that he had said them. He told Jesus more than once, 'No, Lord!'

If somebody is your Lord, you don't ever say 'No' to them. The words that belong together are 'Yes, Lord'.

If you read Acts Chapter 11, you will find out why Peter was saying 'No' and what happened when he realised that this was wrong.

I wonder if you are saying 'No' to the Lord Jesus today? What are you saying 'No' about?

Remember that the words 'Lord' and 'No' are an oxymoron. Jesus doesn't want any oxymorons in your life!

Lord Jesus

We thank you that you have done everything for us. You never said, 'No, Lord' to your Heavenly Father. We pray that you would help us every day to say, 'Yes, Lord Jesus – anything you want, I will do.' We pray this in your name.

Amen.

11. DAVID'S BIG THREE

Lord Jesus,
help me to think about you, learn
more about you, and love you today.

READ: 1 CHRONICLES 11:15-19

What is a drink offering and what does it mean to make your life a 'drink offering'?

Paul wrote about his life being a 'drink offering'.

> *Yes, and if I am being poured out as a drink*
> *offering on the sacrifice and service of your*
> *faith, I am glad and rejoice with you all*
> *(Philippians 2:17).*

Someone else, in the Bible, who offered a drink offering to God was King David.

King David was once forced to live in a cave. People were trying to kill him. So David and some of his friends went to hide in the Cave of Adullam.

Can you imagine what it would have been like living in that cave? They wouldn't have had any electricity or lights. They might have had some smoky old lamps. They certainly wouldn't have had a fridge or freezer. There were no shops or supermarkets near by. And with all the men who were hiding with David, it must have been smelly and stuffy in that cave!

However, the strangest thing of all would have been the people living with David in the cave. Some of David's followers were wild men, strong and fierce. Three of these men were particularly brave. Let's call them 'The Big Three'. They were special friends of David and very loyal to him.

One day David was sitting in the cave. He remembered the well in the little town of Bethlehem where he was born. He remembered how sweet and fresh the water was there. He said out loud, 'Ah, I'd give anything for a drink of water from the well in Bethlehem!'

The Big Three loved David so much that they said to each other, 'Let's go and get him some of that water!' Now Bethlehem was surrounded by their enemies, the Philistines. Any normal soldier would never have made it to the well. But the Big Three managed it!

They made their way past the Philistines and brought back to David a bottle of Bethlehem water. They ran back into the cave shouting, 'David! David! Look what we've got! Look what we've got!'

David thought, 'I can't drink this. These men have risked their lives just to get me a drink of water from Bethlehem. The only thing I can do is give this water to the Lord.'

So, David prayed to God and said, 'Lord, this is the very best I've got and I want you to have it.' Can you believe that he poured the water out?

That's what Paul meant when he spoke about his life being a drink offering. He wanted to give his best to the Lord Jesus. Why? Because Jesus poured out his life as a drink offering to save us.

Lord Jesus

We thank you that you have given to us your very best. Please help us to love and trust you and give to you our very best just as David did. We pray that you will receive the gifts we give for your glory. We pray this in your name.

Amen.

12. JUDAS THE BETRAYER

Lord Jesus,
help me to think about you, learn
more about you, and love you today.

READ: JOHN 13:1–20

What do you do when you have dirty feet or hands? Do you ever wash someone else's dirty feet?

Just before Jesus died, his disciples were with him in a big room. They were going to celebrate the Jewish Passover. However, the disciples were too proud to wash each other's dirty feet. Who do you think washed them instead? Yes, Jesus did.

Jesus then sat down at the table and said, 'One of you is going to let me down and betray me.'

Who betrayed Jesus? It was Judas. He betrayed Jesus for the same amount of money that it would have cost to buy a slave.

How could somebody who had been with Jesus for three years possibly betray him?

Sometimes when you fall you can get a bit of grit or a slither of wood in your hand. Has that ever happened to you? Your mum might then go to the First Aid Box and get out the tweezers. She might not get it all out. What does she do then? She will go to her sewing box and get out a pin. Then she sterilises the pin in boiling water. She uses that pin to try to get the grit out. It's important to get things like that out of your hand. If you don't get the dirt out, your hand might swell up and it could be poisoned.

Something like this happened in Judas' heart. For quite a long time Jesus had been saying to him, 'Judas, there's something I need to get out of your life.'

He'd been teaching Judas and the other disciples that he would need to get all the dirt out of their hearts. Jesus even washed Judas' feet. But he knew that Judas did not want him to wash his heart. Jesus knew that Judas was going to betray him. And that is exactly what Judas did.

How could Judas possibly betray Jesus? Well, there was something in his heart that he wouldn't let Jesus take away.

When I think about that, I ask myself, 'Is there something in my heart that I won't give up to Jesus?' If there is, I need to say, 'Lord Jesus, just take it out of my heart, because I want to love you with all my heart.' I need to say this. And you need to say it too. If you do this you'll live the rest of your life loving and serving him and you'll never, ever, ever become like Judas and betray Jesus.

Lord Jesus

We thank you that you love us. Thank you for showing us when we don't love you. Help us to give over to you anything that would stop us loving you with all our hearts. Be with us we pray, for your sake.

Amen.

13. ON GOD'S SIDE

*Lord Jesus,
help me to think about you, learn
more about you, and love you today.*

READ: JOSHUA 5:13-15

Have you ever seen someone wear a medal? What kind of person would wear a medal?

Athletes sometimes wear medals. But I want you to think about a different sort of medal. In the years 1939-1945 there was a terrible war in Europe and lots of people died. Many men and women did great and brave deeds, and because of their bravery they were awarded medals. There were many battles on the land, in the air, and on the sea during that time.

It is dangerous to be at war. What do you think these soldiers thought of just before they went into battle?

A long, long, time ago Joshua was getting ready to fight a battle against the city of Jericho. He was wondering how his army could defeat this great city. It was going to be a difficult job. Jericho was surrounded by a large, thick wall and there was no way in.

Suddenly, Joshua saw a man standing in front of him dressed for battle with a sword in his hand. If I had been Joshua, I might have turned and run in the other direction! But Joshua stayed to ask the man a question. He could see that he was a soldier. So he asked him, 'Are you on *our* side or are you on *Jericho's* side?'

It was a sensible question, wasn't it? The man was a warrior and he had a sword too. It was important to know whether he was on Joshua's side or whether he was on Jericho's side. But guess what the man said? He said, 'No.'

'Well,' Joshua thought, 'If you're not for Jericho and you're not for us, who are you for?'

This is what the soldier replied, 'I am the Captain of the Lord's army.' Joshua should not have been asking the questions! The Captain was there to find out whose side Joshua was on. Was Joshua on God's side or wasn't he?

Who is the Captain of the Lord's army? Jesus! So whenever you meet with Jesus don't say, 'Are you on my side or are you on their side?' Instead, listen to the question that he asks you, 'Are you on my side?'

Do you have an answer to that question? What would you say? Would you say, 'Yes! Jesus. I'm on your side'? When you are on Jesus' side and you follow him it can be pretty tough going. It is like being in a battle. So, say to Jesus, 'I'm on your side.' Whenever Jesus calls you to be on his side, he will not only lead you – he will also protect you!

Lord Jesus

We thank you today that you are our Captain and that you defend us. You love us and gave your life on the cross to save us. We pray that you would help us day by day to be on your side and to live for your glory. We ask it for your great name's sake.

Amen.

14. SOME NASTY PEOPLE

Lord Jesus,
help me to think about you, learn
more about you, and love you today.

READ: ACTS 13:1-3; ACTS 14:1-7

Sometimes when you start telling people about Jesus they become quite horrible. How does that make you feel?

We are told in the Acts of the Apostles that some people began to get nasty with the Apostle Paul and his friend, Barnabas. Paul and Barnabas were telling them about Jesus. Does that seem strange?

The story of Paul and Barnabas reminds me of a time when I was sixteen years old. I hadn't been a follower of Jesus for all that long. I was really keen to tell others about him. I had a very good friend who was, I think, a little older than I was. He felt the same way I did. We both decided that we had to do something to tell people about Jesus.

Here is what we decided we would do.

We got some books about Jesus, and went to a part of our city where people really needed to hear about him. We thought if we did it near home, somebody might try to stop us! So we went to a part of the city where nobody knew us. It was nerve-racking.

We got there and climbed up some stairs and knocked at a door. When the door opened there was an enormous man who towered above us! He was just a giant! He was huge! I said to him, 'We – we – we – we wondered if you would be interested in a book that would help you to know about Jesus and trust in him.' The man got angry. His face began to go red. He pointed a finger in my face and said, 'If I ever see you and this son of yours ever again, I'll throw you down the stairs!'

I tried to smile at him! I didn't stop to tell him that the friend he had called my son was older than I was!

After the man had slammed the door in our faces, we went back home. We remembered how the Lord Jesus had said, 'If anybody treats you really nastily because you've been trying to tell them about me, I will be with you. You'll have absolutely nothing to fear. I'll fill you with the joy they would have had if they had trusted in me' (See Luke 10: 5-6).

I was sad about what had happened, like Paul and his friends. But Jesus filled my heart with his joy.

Do you have friends who don't know very much about Jesus? I wonder if you could tell them about him. If anybody ever gets nasty with you, remember Jesus' promise. He has said that you'll have double joy because you're serving him!

Lord Jesus

We thank you that you have promised to be with us always. Please give us courage to speak about you and to say that we love you and trust you. We know that you died for us and we know that you're with us. We pray that you would help us to be your witnesses. We pray in your name.

Amen.

15. SOCK BURGERS

*Lord Jesus,
help me to think about you, learn
more about you, and love you today.*

READ: LUKE 18:18–30

A whole family of moths must have been in my cupboard! I used to have some very nice socks, but these socks now have huge holes in them. Now, they have ugly moth holes all over the toes! I left these socks at the back of my cupboard for far too long. Mr and Mrs Moth decided to pay a visit with all their baby moths.

They must have thought that my socks looked like a tasty snack. Moths like to eat things like socks and sweaters. My socks must have seemed to them like a Happy Meal! Sock Burgers were on special offer – super size!

I think it would have been far better if I'd given my socks to someone who needed them. You see I had more socks than I needed. I had forgotten all about these extra ones.

We can be like that, can't we? Even when we don't use something, we don't want to give it to someone else. We say, 'It's mine and nobody else is getting it.'

James, the brother of our Lord Jesus, says, 'When you don't give things to the Lord Jesus, but keep them for yourself, it's like putting your socks in the drawer. The moths will come and eat them all up!'

> Your riches have rotted and your garments
> are moth-eaten (James 5:2 ESV).

If you are not prepared to give things to Jesus then you won't get any pleasure that lasts. I wonder if James knew about the young man that Jesus met one day. This young man had all kinds of good things. But he knew that it was only Jesus who could give him eternal life. So he asked Jesus what he needed to do in order to get eternal life.

Jesus said to him, 'Give away everything you've got to the poor then come and follow me.' Jesus was giving him a test.

The young man was very rich. He had lots of things stored away that he didn't really need. He wasn't using them for anybody else. They weren't doing anybody any good. He wanted to keep them for himself. When Jesus said, 'You come and follow me,' he couldn't leave his things. Even though these things would last only for a short time.

Jesus really liked this young man. He could give him eternal life. But the young ruler went away very sad. He just couldn't bring himself to give his things away – and so he could not hold on to Jesus.

I wonder if you have something tucked away in your heart that you don't want to give to Jesus. Perhaps Jesus is saying to you, 'Give that thing to me so that we can use it together.' The safest thing to do is to give it all to Jesus. Then he'll be happy, you'll be happy and other people will be happy too!

Lord Jesus

You know that we love so many different things and sometimes we hold onto them far too tightly. Help us to give to you everything we have and all that we are, so that we may serve you well. We pray this in your name.

Amen.

16. FAMOUS LAST—AND FIRST—WORDS

Lord Jesus,
help me to think about you, learn
more about you, and love you today.

READ: JOHN 19:28-37

What do you think somebody's last words should be like? At the very least they should be words that you can remember.

A very famous man died whose last words were: 'Two eggs lightly poached.' What a way to die! Well, here are some of my favourite last words. Remember these were the words people spoke just before they died.

James Eades was an engineer. He built things and he made things work. His last words were: 'I cannot die. I've not finished my work.' But then he died.

Alfred Dupont was a very, very, very rich man. He said, 'Thank you, doctors. Thank you, nurses. I'll be gone in a few days.' And then he died.

Spencer Cole was a preacher. He had been preaching through the last book of the Bible. Just before he died he said, 'I should like to finish my exposition of the twenty-second chapter of Revelation.' And then he died. He never finished it – but he saw for himself what it describes!

All these last words have been written down by people who heard them. Last words are supposed to be words that people will remember. But first words can be important too!

In the past, many children used to learn the catechism. A catechism is a small book with lots of questions about God and lots of answers. Years ago, somebody gave me one. The very first question and answer in my catechism was: 'What is the chief end of man?' Here is the wonderful answer: 'Man's chief end is to glorify God and to enjoy him forever.'

What does that mean? The question, 'What is the chief end of man?' means 'What are we really here for?' The answer is 'to glorify God'. That means to love God, to put the Lord Jesus first, and to enjoy him. We are to enjoy loving him and serving him and following him.
I have a New Testament that was given to me when I was a boy. I've kept it because in it I underlined the words that helped me to become a Christian:

Then Jesus spoke to them again, saying, 'I am the light of the world. He who follows Me shall not walk in darkness, but have the light of life' (John 8:12).

When I heard these words I began to trust in the Lord Jesus. He calls you to follow him as well. He promises us, 'I am the light of the world and if you follow me, you will never, ever, ever walk in darkness.'

Will you follow him?

Lord Jesus

Thank you that you love us. Thank you that you can help us to glorify God and to love him and also to enjoy him. Help us to enjoy following you. You are our Light so we will never walk in darkness. We pray this in your wonderful name.

Amen.

17. ARE YOU HAPPY?

*Lord Jesus,
help me to think about you, learn
more about you, and love you today.*

READ: JAMES 5:13-15

Let's ask ourselves a question. Are we happy? Why do we get happy? What makes us happy? In chapter 5 of his book, James, the brother of Jesus asks, 'Is anyone happy?'

> *Is anyone among you suffering? Let him pray. Is anyone cheerful? Let him sing psalms (James 5:13).*

When good things happen to us like holidays, or birthdays – then we are happy.

Some people gave me a lovely plaque with my name on it. Whenever I look at it I think of the Christian friends in South Korea who gave it to me.

I received something else once that made me happy. It was from the boys and girls in our church Sunday school. They drew pictures of themselves and wrote out some Bible verses for me.

So, there are lots of things that make us happy, but what do we do when we're happy? What is it that makes you feel happy? When something makes you happy, you feel like something is rising up inside you – then you smile. The smile rises up inside you and then it pushes out onto your face! You smile because you're happy. Why do we smile? Why do our faces show when we are happy? It's because God made us this way. He gives us all the things and the people that make us happy.

When we're happy, God wants us to have more than just smiley faces. He wants us to share our happiness with others. And he wants us to share it with him.

That's what praising God is all about. When James asked the question, 'Are you happy?' he also made the suggestion 'then why don't you sing?' Singing is another thing we want to do when we are happy.

When you're happy because the Lord Jesus is with you all the time, you can sing to him and say, 'Lord Jesus, I'm so happy because you are so good and kind to me.' Here is something to do when you're on your own in your bedroom or out for a walk. Think about all the good things the Lord Jesus has given you and just sing to him.

The Lord Jesus loves that. There's an amazing verse in the Bible, in the Old Testament, that says God is so happy about having us as his children that he sings about us.

> The LORD your God in your midst,
> The Mighty One, will save;
> He will rejoice over you with gladness,
> He will quiet you with His love,
> He will rejoice over you with singing
> (Zephaniah 3:17).

Are you happy? 'Then,' says James, 'how about singing some songs?'

Lord Jesus

Thank you that you're such a wonderful Saviour and such a wonderful friend. You have given us so many wonderful things to enjoy – our families, friends and our church. We want to sing your praises and thank you for who you are and what you have done. We pray this in your name.

Amen.

Lord Jesus,
help me to think about you, learn
more about you, and love you today.

READ: JOHN 19:25–27

Do you know what an MVP is? An MVP is a Most Valuable Player or Person.

You might award this title to someone who plays best at a football match. But who is the most valuable person to you?

The most valuable person in the world is the Lord Jesus. Who is the next most valuable person?

Before you guess, here are some clues:

1. This MVP tells you hundreds of Bible stories.

2. This MVP changes six thousand nappies.

3. This MVP makes seven thousand dinners.

4. This MVP washes fifteen thousand socks.

5. This MVP says so many prayers for you.

Who do you think this MVP is? Your mum, of course!

Next to the Lord Jesus there is nobody in the world more important than your mum. She has done all these things – the meals, the socks, lots of things for you. She does it because she loves you!

How about giving your mum a great big hug and saying, 'Thank you for loving me. I love you too.'

Or maybe you can tell your dad or your grandma – whoever it is that cares for you and loves you today. Tell them that you are thankful for them and love them very much.

I am thankful for my mum. I'm thankful for those people who have cared for me in the past and who love and care for me today.

I know you are thankful too. Do you ever thank the Lord Jesus for these people?

Lord Jesus

We remember today that you had a mum as well. You loved and cared for her. Even when you were in great pain on the cross, you asked your friend John to look after her. Thank you for our mums. Help us to love them more. We pray this in your name.

Amen.

19. REMEMBER JESUS

Lord Jesus,
help me to think about you, learn
more about you, and love you today.

READ: MATTHEW 26:17–30; 1 CORINTHIANS 10:17

What is a family? Who is in your family? What's it like when you get together? Do you ever think about how you belong to each other? The other people in your family belong to you and you belong to them.

When Christians get together from different parts of the world, they know that they belong to the same family. The disciples knew what this felt like. So did Paul.

On the night before Jesus was going to die, he spent time with his disciples. They had a meal together. Jesus took a loaf of bread and shared it among the disciples. He explained to them that his body would be crucified and that he would die for them.

As the bread was passed around, each disciple took a little bit from the same loaf. This taught them that just as all the bits of bread belonged to one loaf – so all Christians belong in the one family.

Years later, Paul and the other Christians had the same kind of meal. They remembered Jesus and his death.

As they celebrated this special meal, Paul and the other Christians also took a little bit of bread each and ate it together. They all took it from the same loaf.

Paul said, 'Because there is one loaf, we, who are many, are one body, for we all eat of the one loaf.'

This special meal is something that Christians still eat today. They each take a bit of bread from a loaf and eat it. When they do this, they are to remember that each Christian is part of one big group of people.

Every Christian belongs to every other Christian. If you belong to Jesus, then for the rest of your life you will also belong to all the other people in the Christian family all over the world.

That's one of the marvellous and wonderful things about being a Christian.

Loving Heavenly Father

We thank you that we belong to you and to each other. Help us to love other Christians. Help us to love you more because you've given us so many people in your family of love. We thank you for your love and we pray in Jesus' name.

Amen.

20. WHAT THE HEAVENS SAY

Lord Jesus,
help me to think about you, learn
more about you, and love you today.

READ: PSALM 19

What do you see when you look at the sky in the daytime? The sun. Then at night what do you see? The moon. And what else do you see? Stars!

The Bible tells us, 'The heavens declare the glory of God' (Psalm 19:1). That means it's as though the sky, and the marvellous things that are in the sky, are all praising God.

The sun, moon and stars – together they are like a great orchestra. They are all praising God so far away in the sky.

Not everybody hears the music. Not everybody looks up into the sky at night and sees the stars and says, 'They're singing the praises of our Lord Jesus Christ who put all the stars there.' Or 'Look at that great big ball of fire! It's on fire praising God.' Sadly, some people are like radios that have never been 'plugged in' – so they don't hear this music.

So, there's all this wonderful music going on – the stars, and the sun and the moon – they're all praising God. But unless we get 'plugged in' we will not be able to hear. So how do we get 'plugged in'?

We get 'plugged in' when we come to trust in the Lord Jesus who made all these things. He made all that music. When we come and trust in the Lord Jesus, we don't just look up at the sky at night and say, 'Boy, they're far away!' We look up at the sky at night and say, 'Wow! My Saviour Jesus put all these things there so that they could praise him and so that I could look up and know about his power and his love.'

Jesus, God's Son, has made all these wonderful things that we can see through telescopes. He wants us to trust in him because he loves us and cares for us.

Now where do we find out about Jesus? We can only find out about Jesus when we look up at the stars, if first of all we find out about Jesus by looking down at our Bibles!

Loving Lord Jesus

We thank you that you have put the stars in the sky and the Bible in our hands. Help us to trust in you and see the wonderful things that you have done. And as we read your Word, help us to love and praise you for all your power, for all your love and for all your goodness. This we pray in your name.

Amen.

21. JESUS' MUM IN A TIZZY

Lord Jesus,
help me to think about you, learn
more about you, and love you today.

READ: JOHN 2:1-11

Do you know what a tizzy is? I looked up my dictionary to find out what a tizzy was. To be in a tizzy means to be 'in a nervous state'.

Does your mum ever get into a tizzy? Most mums and dads get into a tizzy. Mums get into a tizzy usually when there are just too many things to do. Does your dad get in a tizzy trying to get you ready for school? Does your mum get in a tizzy trying to get everyone ready for church? Nobody likes being late.

One day Jesus, his mum Mary, and some of Jesus' friends were at a wedding. Something happened at this wedding which got Mary in a tizzy.

Have you ever been at a wedding? Did you enjoy it? Weddings are good unless you're in a tizzy. And Jesus' mum was really in a tizzy.

Unlike our weddings, this wedding celebration may have lasted for several days. That was normal in Bible times. Because the celebrations had lasted so long, all the wine ran out before the party was over! That was why Jesus' mum went into a tizzy.

What did she do? She did the first thing you need to do if you're ever in a tizzy – she asked Jesus to help. And then she said something to the people who were there at the wedding. Here are five letters to help you remember just what Jesus' mum said: D W J T Y.

It means *Do What Jesus Tells You*. And that's exactly what they did.

There were huge water containers in the house. Jesus said, 'Fill those containers up with water.' They must have wondered why they were filling them up with water when everybody wanted wine. But they did what Jesus said. They filled them up. Then Jesus told them to pour some out and take it to the person in charge. When they did, the water had turned into wine! The party could go on!

Remember D W J T Y. Whenever you're in a tizzy, do what Jesus tells you!

Lord Jesus

Thank you that you were willing to help out at a wedding when the wine ran out. Help us always to be willing to do whatever you tell us to do, especially when we get in a tizzy with things. We pray in your name.

Amen.

22. WHY DO WE COME TO CHURCH?

Lord Jesus,
help me to think about you, learn
more about you, and love you today.

READ: PSALM 22:22-24

It's nice to see friends, isn't it? Is that one of the reasons that you come to church? But there's another reason, isn't there. We come to meet with the Lord Jesus. My church isn't the only church where Jesus is present with his people. But that's why I come.

Why do we come to meet with Jesus? Well, he has promised us that he will be with us. Jesus said, 'I will be there with you all' (See Matthew 18:20).

What do you think Jesus does during the church services? We can't see him, but we know he's there. Is he just sitting back thinking, 'The singing is not too good today?' Or even, 'That was a pretty average sermon?'

Hebrews chapter 2, verse 12 tells us what Jesus does when he meets with his people!

How does Jesus speak to us in church? Well, he speaks to us when we talk about what he says in the Bible and when the Bible teachers are talking to us about the Lord Jesus.

Have you ever listened to the preacher or Sunday school teacher but felt that at the same time there is another voice that is speaking right into your heart? That's what Jesus says he's doing.

> I will tell of your name to my brothers (Hebrews 2:12 ESV).

So when we come to church, Jesus is the person who does the real preaching and the real teaching.

Jesus also leads our praises. He says:

> ... in the midst of the congregation I will sing your praise (Hebrews 2:12 ESV).

Do you ever share your hymn book with someone in church? You are both looking at the same book so that you can see what words to sing. Now, when we sing together in church it's like singing and sharing our hymn book with Jesus. Jesus is saying, 'Come on, now.

You can praise God better than that. I'm hearing you and I'm leading the worship today!'

So, whenever you come to a church where Jesus also comes to church, listen for his voice and sing together with the Lord Jesus.

Lord Jesus

Thank you that you have promised to be with us and to help us to praise you. We pray that, whenever we meet together as your children, we may be thrilled to know that you have come to bless and help us. We pray this in your name.

Amen.

23. THE EARLY CHURCH

Lord Jesus,
help me to think about you, learn
more about you, and love you today.

READ: ACTS 2:1-13

What do you do in church? What do other people do there? Do some people have certain jobs to do? What do they do in your church when some things are not getting done?

After Judas had betrayed Jesus, there were eleven apostles left. But altogether there were about 120 disciples of Jesus in Jerusalem. On the day of Pentecost, another 3,000 people became Christians. That's 120 plus 3,000. Then later on we are told how many men were in the church. Just counting the men, the number came to 5,000. But the church wasn't just made up of men. There would have been women and children too. So we can see from these numbers that the church was growing. More and more people were trusting in Jesus.

Now, let's imagine that if there were 5,000 men there would have been about 5,000 women and they perhaps had about two children each. So you multiply 5,000 by 4 which is 20,000.

So there were probably 20,000 people in the Jerusalem church. They met in homes. How many people do you think could meet together in a big house? I suppose a really big house with a garden could have about 300 people.

So let's say there were 300 in each church. How many 300s are there in 20,000? You will need to get out your calculator to work out this sum. The number you get will be 66.666. That's sixty-seven churches! The apostles did the preaching and teaching in these sixty-seven churches. At first there were only eleven apostles. So each apostle must have had to teach in at least six churches. Many of these churches were meeting every day, so perhaps the eleven apostles were teaching every day in all sixty-seven churches. That's a lot of teaching!

On top of that, they had to organise all these churches. So one day the apostles said, 'We're going to get some other people to do things in our churches.' And that's what they did. They said, 'We can't do everything – we're not the only Christians here. We need to get other people involved.'

So they looked for people who were filled with the Spirit of Jesus and said, 'Let's get these people involved.'

What do you think happened next? They actually ended up with even more churches than before! Why was this? It's simple – other people were now involved. It's like that in every church. It's wrong to think that the minister should do everything. Everybody in the church should be doing something.

Is there something you can do?

Loving Heavenly Father

We give you thanks for the blessings that you give to us. We thank you that you have given to some people the gift of speaking, to others the gift of helping, and to some the gift of organising. We pray in Jesus' name.

Amen.

24. SEE ME SEE THE FATHER

Lord Jesus,
help me to think about you, learn
more about you, and love you today.

READ: JOHN 14:9–14

I have a friend whose name is David. He is a small man who wears spectacles. He is very clever and very serious. He always gets straight to the point.

One day I was in a church in the same country that my friend David comes from. I was standing at the front of the church and saw someone walking towards me. He was a small man with round spectacles. When he came and spoke to me, he was very serious and he got straight to the point! Do you know what I said to him? 'You must be my friend David's father.'

He said, 'How did you know?'

Well, I couldn't say, 'Because you're small, you wear round spectacles, you're very serious and you get straight to the point,' could I? But that was the truth! Because I knew David, as soon as I saw this man and saw his spectacles, and heard him speak, I knew this must be David's father.

This reminded me of what Jesus said, 'If you have seen me, if you know me, if you know what I am like, then you know exactly what my Heavenly Father is like' (See John 14:7).

One day I was waiting at a train station. There was a man standing near me. I could hardly believe it. He looked just like a friend of mine. His face looked just the same, his hair was the same – he was jingling coins in his pocket just like my friend used to do, and he was whistling. My friend always whistled.

I stood and looked at him and thought to myself, 'He looks exactly like my friend, only a little bit older.'

I wondered, 'Will I or won't I?' 'Will I or won't I?'

Quietly, I walked over towards him. Then I was standing right next to him.

I asked him if he was the brother of my friend.

And he said, 'Yes.'

It was his brother! How did I know it was his brother? Because he was so like his brother, my friend.

We know what our Heavenly Father is like because we know Jesus. Other people also discover what Jesus is like when they see us getting more and more like him. We are in Jesus' family, and we remind people of him! Wouldn't it be wonderful if your friends began to think about the Lord Jesus because they saw that you are like him?

Lord Jesus

Thank you that you've shown us your Heavenly Father and that by your Spirit you are able to make us more like you, our dear elder brother. We pray that you would do this so that others may know that we belong to your family and will want to belong to it too. We ask this in your name.

Amen.

25. WHO SHOULD WE WORSHIP?

Lord Jesus,
help me to think about you, learn
more about you, and love you today.

READ: 1 SAMUEL 12:21

If you were going to describe yourself, what words would you use? What do you look like? What things are you good at? What foods do you enjoy? We're all different, different shapes and sizes.

Isn't that marvellous! What an amazing God made us! And all the more amazing because he sent the Lord Jesus to be our Saviour and our Friend and our Lord. He is the one we are to love most of all. This is why we worship him and sing praises to him and say, 'Oh, you're a great God. You do wonderful things.' So, here's a question for you. Is there anything in your heart that takes the place of God and do you ever say to that person or thing, 'Oh, you are wonderful and I want you more than anything else in the world!'?

That would be silly, wouldn't it? But that is what we are like. Sometimes we are silly. Have you ever seen people who get new cars and they're out every day polishing their new car? They wouldn't think about praising God and thanking God and loving God and saying, 'I want to take care of your Kingdom and I want to serve you.' Instead, in their hearts, they're saying, 'Oh car, you are the most wonderful thing in the world!'

Or they think about their money in the bank and it's as though they are saying, 'Oh, great money in the bank – I love you and you are wonderful and you can do wonderful things for me!'

Perhaps it's football that you think about the most or golf, or hockey or getting ninety-nine percent at school. Oh, that's going to make all the difference!

Because we've got such sinful hearts and such foolish heads, we worship all kinds of things instead of worshipping the true and living God.

Think about what he has done, how he has created the world, and how he keeps the world going. Do you ever see these programmes on television that tell you how big the universe is? Imagine the mind that thought that up and keeps it going. The same God who does that, knows you and me by name! And he loves us.

Remember that. There is nothing else that we can make or that we can do that we should worship.

Loving Heavenly Father

We thank you that you are the true and living God. Help us to discover day by day that you are a wonderful friend and a great God who deserves to be worshipped and loved and praised and followed. Keep us from falling into temptation and help us to serve you every day. We ask it for your great name's sake.

Amen.

Lord Jesus,
help me to think about you, learn
more about you, and love you today.

READ: 1 THESSALONIANS 1:1-10

Do you know what a model is? Perhaps you've seen one at a fashion show. When someone is called a model, what might they be doing?

Paul said to the Christians in Thessalonika that their little church had become a model to other churches. It was still quite small with not that many people in it, but it had become a church that others were to copy.

If you hear about a model in the news or on the internet you are usually hearing about someone who walks around in really expensive clothes. They strut around on something called a catwalk and people who look at what they're wearing say, 'Wow! That looks good. That looks really good! I think I'd like that.'

Now, it looks easy being a model but there are all kinds of things that you need to be able to do if you're a model. You need to be able to walk in a certain way and you need to be able to wear clothes in a certain way.

Perhaps you're still not convinced.

Well, I once had to get something done to my back and the physiotherapist said, 'Just sit up straight with your head straight.' I tried to do that and she sighed and said, 'Do you think that's straight?' I didn't find that easy.

Models have to know how to stand straight. They've got to be able to have every part of their body working properly. So that when people see the beautiful clothes they are wearing, they think, 'Wow! I think that looks lovely. I would look great in that!'

The Lord Jesus Christ wants us to be a model church so that people who do not yet trust in the Saviour or love him, will look at us and say, 'Wow! It must be something to belong there!'

And if we're going to be a model church, then every part of the body of Jesus, which is what Paul also calls the church, must work properly together.

In a body there are big bits and little bits. It's the same in the church. We've got people who are bigger and people who are smaller. And when the smaller bits as well as the bigger bits are living for the Lord Jesus, then people say 'Wow! It must be wonderful to belong to the church. Their Lord and Saviour would be worth following.'

Are you one of the bigger people or one of the smaller people? That doesn't matter. You are important to the church whether you are the smallest or the tallest. So So here is what to say to the Lord Jesus, 'Lord Jesus, I want to love you and trust you as my Saviour and serve you as my Lord so that people will say, 'My, that's a model church that they belong to!'

Lord Jesus

We thank you that you have called us to follow you and to be your disciples and your friends. We thank you that we are not only your friends but we are each other's friends. We pray that you would help us to love each other, to be with each other, to enjoy each other because of all you have done for us. We pray this in your name.

Amen.

27. GOOFING IT UP

Lord Jesus,
help me to think about you, learn
more about you, and love you today.

READ: GENESIS 22:1-19

Do you know what it means to 'goof it up'? It means
that you make a terrible mess of things.

There were some people in the early church who goofed
up the gospel by saying, 'If you are really going to be
a Christian then you need to do the things that the
Jewish people did.' These things were like the Holy days
and the different kinds of foods that you could eat and
not eat.

Some people said, 'If you really are going to be a
Christian you need to do all these other things.' But
people like Paul said, 'No. If you really are going to be a
Christian the thing you need to do is to trust in the Lord
Jesus, because he died to take away all our sins.'

Some other people said, 'Well, I trust in Jesus.' But they never showed it by being obedient, by doing things the Lord Jesus said. So James, who was one of the ministers in the church in Jerusalem, told his listeners about something God had said to Abraham: 'Now Abraham you said you trusted me, you really trusted me. I want you to take your only son, Isaac, and I want you to go and sacrifice him on top of a mountain.'

Abraham replied, 'You said you would bless me. You didn't tell me it was going to be this hard.'

God said to Abraham, 'Abraham if you trust me you will do the things I say.'

When James told the people that story he was trying to help them understand that when we trust in Jesus we will do the things he says. Jesus tells us to help the people who are poor and needy, and to make friends with people who are alone. If we don't then we're not really trusting in him – not at all. So, if we are to really trust in Jesus we will want to do the things that Jesus tells us to do.

Now, sometimes people wear T-shirts with the slogan on them, 'Just do it.'

I think we should wear T-shirts like that in church.

Because we trust the Lord Jesus and we love him we are to show that we trust him by doing things that please him and that help others. We don't do that in order to become Christians, do we? We 'just do it' because we trust in him.

Trusting the Lord Jesus will help us not to 'goof it up'.

Lord Jesus

Sometimes you ask us to show that we trust you by doing things that are hard for us. Please fill us with love for you and love for others so that we can serve you more. Bless us today so that we can learn more about you and love and trust you more, and serve you better. This we ask for your sake.

Amen.

Lord Jesus,
help me to think about you, learn
more about you, and love you today.

READ: JAMES 1:5; 1 KINGS 4:29-30; PSALM 111:10

Let me tell you something that might make you smile!

I came across some notes of a sermon I once preached in church when I was a very young man. I don't think I kept the sermon notes because it was such a good sermon! No. The really interesting thing about these notes is that there are some words written on the top of the sermon that were not part of the sermon.

I had a friend who used to say to me, 'You are a wise old owl. But when you preach you do not smile very much. When you preach I want you to do this. I want you to write at the top of the very first sermon, "Even an old owl would smile".' That set me thinking. We often speak about owls as wise. However, if you have ever seen an owl, they look as if they are smiling all the time.

But why would an owl smile?

Is this the answer? An owl smiles because it is a wise old owl. And if you are a wise old owl or a wise young owl, you can smile because you are wise.

What does it mean to be wise? It means, first of all, that you love God, that you trust God, and that you know that everything God is doing in your life is to bless you and help you, to love you and to make you more like Jesus.

So, whatever happens you can keep smiling because your God is in control of everything. Isn't that amazing? Even when something happens that hurts you, that is sore, you can be wise and say, 'My heavenly Father knows exactly what he is doing.'

When you become wise like that, the Bible tells you (in Psalm 119:96, 99) that you can be wiser than the people who teach you and wiser than your enemies. When someone hurts you you can say 'Oh, that does hurt, but my Heavenly Father knows what he is doing.'

So, even though I'm not a wise old owl, I hope I have become a wiser Christian! And the way to become a wiser old Christian is by first becoming a wiser young Christian. And the Bible can teach you how to do that.

Loving Heavenly Father

You are so wise in everything you do and so loving. We thank and praise you that even though there are things in our lives we don't understand, and people who hurt us, you know what you are doing. We can smile up at you in faith and in love and trust you to do us good. We praise you for your love, in Jesus' name.

Amen.

29. WHERE'S YOUR BODYGUARD?

Lord Jesus,
help me to think about you, learn
more about you, and love you today.

READ: EXODUS 20:1-17

Here's a question for you. Are you any good at guessing what people do from the way they dress? Can you recognise where a person is from by the clothes they wear? For instance do people from America wear special clothes? Or do people from Scotland wear different clothes to people from other countries?

Could you recognise what job someone did by the clothes they wore? For example, a policeman? I think you would recognise them by their uniform, perhaps by their hat or the badges they wear.

If you saw a bodyguard what other clothes might they wear? Would they carry special equipment? A bodyguard might carry a gun and wear a transmitter in his ear to communicate with other bodyguards.

But what is a bodyguard for? The president of the United States has bodyguards. When President Reagan was president of the United States, somebody tried to shoot him. A bodyguard threw himself in front of him and got shot because that's what bodyguards are for. That's why they're called 'bodyguards', because they are there to protect the bodies of very important people.

Now God has given all of us ten bodyguards and they are called the Ten Commandments. You can find these in the book of Exodus Chapter 20 in the Bible.

> You shall have no other gods before me.
>
> You shall not make for yourself a carved image.
>
> You shall not take the name of the LORD your God in vain.
>
> Remember the Sabbath day, to keep it holy.
>
> Honour your father and your mother.
>
> You shall not murder.
>
> You shall not commit adultery.
>
> You shall not steal.
>
> You shall not bear false witness against your neighbour.
>
> You shall not covet your neighbour's house … nor anything that is your neighbour's.

God gave us these commands because with these bodyguards we'll be safe as we serve and love the Lord.

Loving Heavenly Father

Thank you that you want to protect us. Help us always to hide your Word in our hearts that we might not sin against you. Thank you for your love. We pray in Jesus' name.

Amen.

Lord Jesus,
help me to think about you, learn
more about you, and love you today.

READ: REVELATION 3:20

There was once a church that was celebrating the Lord's Supper, but something or someone was missing? Can you guess what?

> Behold, I stand at the door and knock. If anyone hears My voice and opens the door, I will come in to him and dine with him, and he with Me (Revelation 3:20).

Those were the words that Jesus spoke when he knocked on the door of that church. If Jesus was having to knock on the door of the church from the outside, what was missing in that church when they were going to have the Lord's Supper? How could they have the Lord's Supper with Jesus, if he was on the outside?

Jesus was knocking at the door of that church and saying, 'I want to be there with you when you have the Lord's Supper.' Isn't that a strange thing? This church was going to have the Lord's Supper and Jesus hadn't been invited.

Wouldn't it be a strange thing if we called ourselves Christians and we had never invited Jesus into our lives?

Jesus says: 'I am standing at the door and knocking. If anyone will open the door, I will come in and we will spend our lives together.'

Now, I've a question for you, have you ever heard Jesus knocking and saying to you, 'I want to come into your life. I want to be your Saviour and your Lord.' If you have, then the thing to do is to say, 'Lord Jesus, come in and be my Saviour.'

When we take the bread and the wine in church, that is what we are really saying. The bread is a sign that Jesus' body was sacrificed for us on the cross. He did this because he loves us.

The wine is a sign that Jesus poured out his blood so that our sins could be forgiven. When we take the bread and the wine, we're saying to the Lord Jesus. 'We want to be yours.'

Let's pray that we'll love him that way.

Lord Jesus

We thank you that you want to come to us, that you want to be our Saviour, our Friend and our Lord. We pray that you would help us to give our hearts to you and to trust you and to love you and to serve you. Please Lord Jesus, don't stay outside of our lives, but come in and be our Friend. We ask this in your name.

Amen.

31. DO ANGELS HAVE NAMES?

Lord Jesus,
help me to think about you, learn
more about you, and love you today.

READ: ISAIAH 6:1-7

Do angels have names? Yes. How many angels' names do you know? Because we know a few angels' names, does that mean every angel has a name? You would think so, wouldn't you?

Angels do have names and there are two different kinds of names for angels, just as we have two different kinds of names. We've got family names (surnames) and Christian names (first names). Angels are a bit like that because we know that God has made them in different families.

Right at the beginning of the Bible we read about angels called 'cherubim'. Do you know what they were holding in their hands? They were holding flaming swords that were turning in different directions to guard the way to the Garden of Eden. They were powerful. And then there is another family called the 'seraphim'. So there are cherubs and seraphs. We read about seraphs in Isaiah chapter 6. They are also very powerful.

God has a great angel whose name is Gabriel. His name means, 'God is great'. Now if Gabriel appeared this morning, do you think you would say, 'Hey there Gabriel, how's it going?' No, because he is an angel and angels are great. Although God made his angels as well as making us, they are very different from us.

God made angels to be servants of his church and so even when we don't see angels, they are often doing things to serve God's people.

The Bible tells us quite a lot about angels, but one of the most important things we need to know is that God uses them to watch over his people. Sometimes something will happen to you and you'll think, I wonder if God sent an angel to protect me there?

The Lord Jesus is our King and he is the King of the angels too. Let's pray to him right now.

Lord Jesus

You use your angels to serve your people. And you also use your people to serve each other. We want to serve you with all our hearts and we pray that you would help us to do this. We ask this in your name.

Amen.

Conclusion

Well, you have made it right to the end of the book! Well done! I hope you have enjoyed it and that it has helped you to think about the Lord Jesus, to trust him, and to love him more.

Most of the books I have written are for grown-ups. So why does someone who writes for grown-ups want to write books for children as well? There are lots of reasons, but since we're at the end of the book now, maybe I should mention only two.

The first is that when the Lord Jesus was on earth, he loved children and children loved him. And that's still true! He wants you to know that and he wants you to trust him as your Saviour and love him as your Lord. Books about him can help us to do that. I hope this one has helped you.

The second reason is this. Although I am a grown-up, I was once one of the children who needed to learn about Jesus' love for me. And so, when I was your age, I started reading the Bible each day, and asking the Lord to help me to understand it. I hope you will do the same. The Bible is a big book—actually there are sixty-six books in it—and I needed help to read it and understand it. Two books you might find helpful are *66 Books One Story* and *Read With Me*.[1]

---

1. Paul Reynolds, *66 Books One Story*, (Christian Focus Publications, Tain, Ross-shire, Scotland, 2013) ISBN: 978-1-84550-819-7.
Jean Stapleton, *Read With Me*, (Christian Focus Publications, Tain, Ross-shire, Scotland, 2006) ISBN: 978-1-84550-148-8.

So I hope you will start reading the Bible when you are young. But try not to make the mistake I did! I thought that reading the Bible each day was the same thing as being a Christian. It was a while before I realised that although that's important, it's not the same as knowing and trusting the Lord Jesus himself. Then, one day, I was reading the words of Jesus in John's Gospel chapter 5 verses 39-40. He said to some people who were listening to him: 'You search the Scriptures, for in them you think you have eternal life; and these are they which testify of Me. But you are not willing to come to Me that you may have life.' I realised that Jesus was not just speaking to people long ago who made that mistake. I had made it too. He was speaking to me!

I knew then that I must pray that he would help me to come to him, to trust him, and to get to know him. Some time later, Jesus' words in John's Gospel Chapter 8, verse 12 helped me to do that: 'Then Jesus spoke to them again, saying, "I am the light of the world. He who follows Me shall not walk in darkness, but have the light of life".' He has kept his promise!

So now you know why I wanted to write this book! And now I hope you will want to read the very best book—the Bible—yourself. Maybe you could start by reading John's Gospel.

May you know the love and presence of the Lord Jesus every day!

Sinclair B. Ferguson

Sinclair uses the tried-and-tested method of question-and-answer catechesis to lead our children in a warm-hearted devotion to Christ. Another great book to help our children spend time thinking about how Jesus cares for them.

Jonny Gibson
Associate Professor of Old Testament,
Westminster Theological Seminary;
Author of *The Moon Is Always Round*

Parents and grandparents will love reading these delightful and inspiring devotions to their beloved children and grandchildren. Each page is filled with engaging and fun stories that help children learn about the many ways Jesus cares for them. This devotional book not only teaches them about Jesus but helps them to love Jesus as they learn to rest in Jesus and his eternal care for them.

Burk Parsons
Senior Pastor of Saint Andrew's Chapel
and Editor of Tabletalk Magazine

TRUTHFORLIFE®

THE BIBLE-TEACHING MINISTRY OF **ALISTAIR BEGG**

The mission of Truth For Life is to teach the Bible with clarity and relevance so that unbelievers will be converted, believers will be established, and local churches will be strengthened.

Daily Program

Each day, Truth For Life distributes the Bible teaching of Alistair Begg across the U.S. and in several locations outside of the U.S. through 2,000 radio outlets. To find a radio station near you, visit **truthforlife.org/stationfinder**.

Free Teaching

The daily program, and Truth For Life's entire teaching library of over 3,000 Bible-teaching messages, can be accessed for free online at **truthforlife.org** and through Truth For Life's mobile app, which can be download for free from your app store.

At-Cost Resources

Books and audio studies from Alistair Begg are available for purchase at cost, with no markup. Visit **truthforlife.org/store**.

Where to Begin?

If you're new to Truth For Life and would like to know where to begin listening and learning, find starting point suggestions at **truthforlife.org/firststep**. For a full list of ways to connect with Truth For Life, visit **truthforlife.org/subscribe**.

Contact Truth For Life

P.O. Box 398000 Cleveland, Ohio 44139
phone 1 (888) 588-7884   **email** letters@truthforlife.org
truthforlife.org

Christian Focus Publications publishes books for adults and children under its four main imprints: Christian Focus, CF4K, Mentor and Christian Heritage. Our books reflect our conviction that God's Word is reliable and Jesus is the way to know him, and live for ever with him.

Our children's publication list covers pre-school to early teens. We also publish personal and family devotional titles, biographies and inspirational stories that children will love.

From pre-school board books to teenage apologetics, we have it covered!

Christian Focus Publications Ltd,
Geanies House, Fearn, Ross-shire,
IV20 1TW, Scotland,
United Kingdom.
www.christianfocus.com